D0603949

Math All Around

Division with Toys

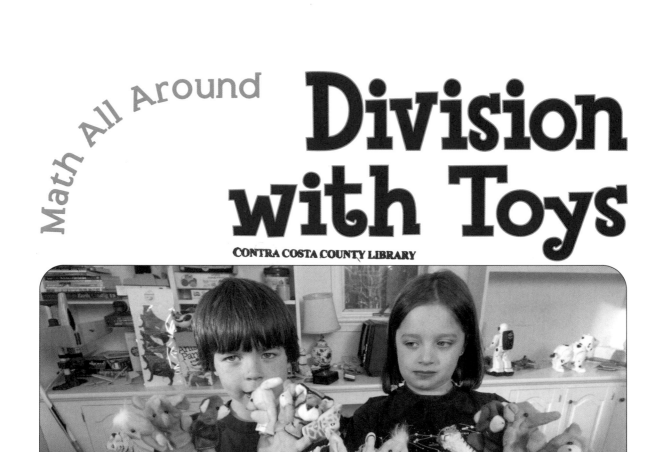

Jennifer Rozines Roy and Gregory Roy

Marshall Cavendish

It's a rainy day and you and your friends are stuck inside. But you can still play indoor games! There are lots of toys in your playroom.

You start with the race cars. This box has ten cars inside. If you were alone, you could play with all the cars yourself. But your friend wants to play cars, too.

The two of you can share the cars. How will you make it fair?

Give one car to your friend then take one for yourself. Pick another car for you and another for your friend. Do this until the box is empty.

You've divided the cars into two groups. Each of you has five cars. Now that's fair!

Would you like to play with marbles? You'll need to **divide** them, too. When you divide, you separate things into groups.

If each of you takes the same number of marbles, there will be two groups of fifteen.

Here comes another friend. She also wants to play. To make the game fair, you will need to divide the marbles into three groups.

Put all the marbles back together in one group and get ready to divide them again.

Pick one marble for you, one for your friend, and one for your other friend.

Choose another for you, another for your friend, and one more for your other friend.

Keep doing this until all the marbles are handed out.

Thirty marbles can be divided into three equal groups. Each group has ten marbles.

Grab your ten marbles and start shooting!

Let's color pictures! You have twelve colored markers. If you divide them, everyone can draw.

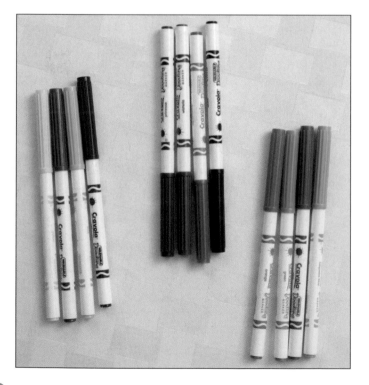

Twelve markers divided by three friends equals four markers apiece.

We can write this as a **division** fact. There are two ways to write division facts. But, they say the same thing: twelve divided by three equals four.

$$12 \div 3 = 4$$

divided by

equals

$$3\overline{)12} 4$$

equals

divided by

What beautiful pictures!

What do you want to do next? Let's go check out the video games.

Both controllers are being used.

2 controllers **÷ 2** friends **= 1** controller each

$$2 \div 2 = 1 \qquad 2\overline{)\,2}^{\,1}$$

When a number is divided by itself, it always equals one.

Only one person can use each controller at a time, so you'll have to find something else to do.

You decide to build something. Here's a box of Legos.

This box has forty Legos. You dump them all out. Divide them into three groups for three children.

Each group has thirteen Legos. That's fair. But there's still one Lego left over. Forty Legos didn't divide evenly into three groups.

The one left over is called the **remainder**. The division fact can be written:

$$40 \div 3 = 13 \text{ R1} \qquad 3\overline{)40}^{\,13 \text{ R1}}$$

"R" stands for remainder.

It's okay to have a remainder. You can still play. But what if you wanted to divide the Legos and have none left over?

What could you do to make forty Legos divide into **equal** groups? You could ask a friend to join you!

If there are four children, each person can
have ten Legos.

$$40 \div 4 = 10 \qquad 4\overline{)40}^{\,10}$$

A couple of your friends are setting up a beanbag toss. There are twelve beanbags. Each player gets two beanbags.

How many children can play the game?

12 beanbags ÷ **2** beanbags = **6** players

$$12 \div 2 = 6 \qquad 2\overline{)12}^{\,6}$$

You and three friends can join the game. Grab two beanbags and get in line.

One by one, everybody takes a turn. Six kids throw two beanbags each.

That sounds like a multiplication fact!

6 kids **x** **2** beanbags **=** **12** beanbags

Did you know that multiplication is the opposite of division?

When you divide, you separate things into groups.

10 race cars ÷ **2** = **5** race cars in **2** groups

30 marbles ÷ **3** = **10** marbles in **3** groups

12 markers ÷ **3** = **4** markers in **3** groups

When you multiply, you put the groups together.
5 race cars **x 2** = **10** race cars
10 marbles **x 3** = **30** marbles
4 markers **x 3** = **12** markers

After the game is finished, you and three friends put on a puppet show.

There are twenty finger puppets and four hand puppets. How many different ways can you divide up the puppets?

20 ÷ 4 = 5

$20 \div 2 = 10$

$4 \div 2 = 2$

$20 \div 4 = 5$

$4 \div 4 = 1$

You have time to play one more game before supper. Would you like to play checkers?

Two people can play checkers. There are twenty-four checkers. The checkers are divided into two sets, one for each player.

One set is white. The other set is black. How many checkers are in each set?

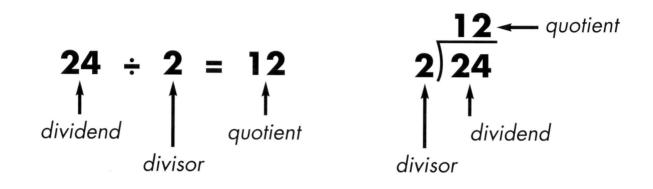

$$24 \div 2 = 12$$

dividend divisor quotient

$$2\overline{)24} = 12 \leftarrow quotient$$

divisor dividend

In a division fact, the whole amount is called the **dividend**. Here, twenty-four is the dividend.

The number we are dividing by is called the **divisor**. Two is the divisor, because there are two different colored sets of checkers.

The answer to a division fact is called the **quotient**. Twelve is the quotient. Each player gets twelve checkers to jump across the board.

Game over! It's time to clean up. Cleaning up is quicker and easier when you divide the chores between friends. Get to work!

Glossary

divide — To separate into groups.

dividend — A number that is divided by another number.

division — The process of finding out how many times one number goes into another number.

divisor — A number by which another number is divided.

equal — Being the same in amount, size, value, or other quality.

quotient — The answer to a division fact.

remainder — The number that is left over in a division fact; must be less than the divisor.

Read More

Caron, Lucille and Philip M. St. Jacques. *Multiplication and Division*. Enslow, 2001.

Lobb, Janice. *Color and Noise: Let's Play with Toys*. Kingfisher, 2001.

Long, Lynette. *Dazzling Division: Games and Activities that Make Math Easy and Fun*. Jossey-Bass, 2000.

Napoli, Donna Jo and Richard Tchen. *How Hungry Are You?* Atheneum, 2001.

Web Sites

AAAKnow Math: Division
www.aaaknow.com/div.htm

A+ Math
www.aplusmath.com/flashcards/division.html

Dositey Division
www.dositey.com/muldiv/div.htm

Index

Page numbers in **boldface** are illustrations.

About the Authors

Jennifer Rozines Roy is the author of more than twenty books. A former Gifted and Talented teacher, she holds degrees in psychology and elementary education.

Gregory Roy is a civil engineer who has co-authored several books with his wife. The Roys live in upstate New York with their son Adam.

Marshall Cavendish Benchmark
99 White Plains Road
Tarrytown, New York 10591-9001
www.marshallcavendish.us

Library of Congress Cataloging-in-Publication Data

Roy, Jennifer Rozines, 1967–
Division with toys / by Jennifer Rozines Roy and Gregory Roy.
p. cm. — (Math all around)
Summary: "Applies division skills to playtime, stimulates critical thinking,
and provides students with an understanding of math in the real world"—Provided by publisher.
Includes bibliographical references and index.
ISBN-13: 978-0-7614-2269-3
ISBN-10: 0-7614-2269-2
1. Division—Juvenile literature. I. Roy, Gregory. II. Title.
III. Series: Roy, Jennifer Rozines, 1967– Math all around.
QA115.R6855 2006
513.2'14—dc22
2006010307

Photo Research by Anne Burns Images

Cover Photo by *Jay Mallin Photos*

The photographs in this book are used with permission and through the courtesy of:
Jay Mallin Photos: pp. 1, 2, 4, 5LR, 6TB, 7, 8, 9, 10LR, 11, 12, 14TB, 15, 17, 18LR, 20, 21(all), 22, 23(all), 24, 27.

Series design by Virginia Pope

Printed in Malaysia
1 3 5 6 4 2